How It Is Made

Cocoa to Chocolate

B.J. Best

Cavendish
Square

New York

Published in 2017 by Cavendish Square Publishing, LLC
243 5th Avenue, Suite 136, New York, NY 10016

Library of Congress Cataloging-in-Publication Data

Names: Best, B. J., 1976- author.
Title: Cocoa to chocolate / B.J. Best.
Description: New York: Cavendish Square Publishing, [2017] | Series: How it is made
Identifiers: LCCN 2016029417 (print) | LCCN 2016031738 (ebook) |
ISBN 9781502621306 (pbk.) | ISBN 9781502621313 (6 pack) | ISBN 9781502621320 (library bound) | ISBN 9781502621337 (ebook)
Subjects: LCSH: Chocolate processing--Juvenile literature. | Cocoa processing--Juvenile literature. | Chocolate--Juvenile literature.
Classification: LCC TP640 .B47 2017 (print) | LCC TP640 (ebook) | DDC 664--dc23
LC record available at https://lccn.loc.gov/2016029417

Editorial Director: David McNamara
Copy Editor: Rebecca Rohan
Associate Art Director: Amy Greenan
Designer: Alan Sliwinski
Production Coordinator: Karol Szymczuk
Photo Research: J8 Media

The photographs in this book are used by permission and through the courtesy of: Cover (left) Mchin/Shutterstock.com, (right) Al1962/Shutterstock.com; p. 5 Apic/Hulton Archive/Getty Images; p. 7 Yakov Oskanov/Shutterstock.com; p. 9 Dwart/iStockphoto.com; p. 11 Christopher Jones/Alamy Stock Photo; p. 13 Georgia Glynn Smith/Getty Images; p. 15 Tracey Kusiewicz/Foodie Photography/Getty Images; p. 17 Valentyn Volkov/Shutterstock.com; p. 19 Hemis/Alamy Stock Photo; p. 21 seyephoto/Shutterstock.com.

Printed in the United States of America

Contents

People have eaten chocolate for hundreds of years.

At first, it was a bitter drink.

5

Chocolate begins on a tree.

It is called a **cacao** tree.

This tree grows pods.

Inside the pods are
white beans.

The beans are dried.

They change color.

9

The beans are shipped
to a factory.

They are shipped in sacks.

11

The beans are **roasted**.

This cracks the shell on the bean.

13

The shell is removed.

The bean is now called a nib.

15

The nibs are ground. Then they are **pressed**.

This makes cocoa powder and cocoa butter.

Sugar is added to the powder and butter.

The chocolate **liquid** is mixed in a large **vat**.

The chocolate liquid
is shaped.

It cools and becomes hard.

Then it is packaged and
ready to eat!

New Words

cacao (kuh-KOW) The tree where cocoa beans grow.

liquid (LIHK-wid) Something that flows.

pressed (PRESSED) Pushed and made flat by weight.

roasted (ROH-sted) Cooked with heat.

vat (VAT) A large tub.

Index

23

About the Author

B.J. Best lives in Wisconsin with his wife and son. He has written several other books for children. He likes dark chocolate.

About

Bookworms help independent readers gain reading confidence through high-frequency words, simple sentences, and strong picture/text support. Each book explores a concept that helps children relate what they read to the world they live in.